KINDLE FIRE HD 8&10 ADVANCED USER GUIDE

Step-by-Step Instructions To
Enrich Your FIRE HD Experience!

TABLE OF CONTENTS

INTRODUCTION

The new Amazon Kindle Fire HD 8 and 10 are tablets that are meant to help you do a variety of activity through just one electronic device. It can be somewhat difficult to understand and setup everything on a new device; this book provides all the information that you need to not only understand your Kindle Fire HD device but also about using it in a more productive manner.

The flow of the book will help you understand your device from the basics, including things like the controls and buttons while at the same time telling you about all the other activities that you can do on your Kindle. This book is your guide for making better use of this device; even if you're a person who has a good amount of knowledge on this device, you'll still find this book useful as it's filled with helpful tips and shortcuts.

All the information in this book has been simplified so that it's easier for you to understand what you're doing; the information has been compiled in such a manner that you can easily find what you want.

There is so much that you can do with your tablet, from readings books, using the internet, watching movies and to listening to your favorite music, this book is all you need to understand all the activities that you can do on your Kindle.

Therefore, you can sit back and relax because this book will teach you all that you need to master your Kindle.

Chapter 1:

BASICS

The Amazon Kindle Fire HD 8 and 10 are incredible devices that can fulfill all your needs if you know how to make use of them properly. Before we begin with setting up of your device, there are a few basics that you should be aware of in regards to the tablet. This chapter will tell you all about the Kindle Fire HD including specifications and comparisons with other devices in the market.

What is Kindle Fire HD Tablet

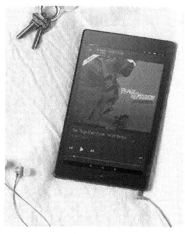

The Kindle Fire HD Tablet is your basic touch-screen tablet that you can use to do a lot of interesting things. It's been designed by Amazon and comes with an operating system built by Google specifically for this tablet; Kindle Fire HD tablet is more convenient than any other electronic device that you can use. It's straightforward and compact so you can easily carry it anywhere, but at the same time, it has a pretty good screen resolution so that you can fully enjoy whatever you are doing.

Kindle Fire HD tablet can be used to read books; it has been specifically built to improve your reading experience, plus it's way easier to store all your books on the tablet and read them whenever and wherever you want. The tablet can do any other thing that you might want, such as using the internet for any of your needs; you can even use social media sites like Facebook or Twitter. You can watch movies, TV shows or listen to the music of your choice and you can even play games on it.

The tablet at the end of the day makes your life so much easier because you can perform all these different activities by using just one device and at the same time it's not as expensive as other devices like the laptops. Hence it's the perfect thing to buy that can satisfy all your requirements.

Device Specification for HD 8 and 10

These two devices that Amazon has launched are similar in usage, however they do have slightly different specifications.

Kindle Fire HD 8

Price: $89.99 for 16GB and $119.99 for 32GB

Color: It comes in 4 colors- Black, Blue, Magenta and Tangerine

Screen: It has an 8-inch widescreen (1280x800 pixels) HD display that comes with over a million pixels (189 ppm).

Performance: It comes with Quad-core 1.3 GHz processor, and the RAM is 1.5 GB.

Storage: It comes with 16GB/32GB, but you can store up to

200GB with the support of a MicroSD card. It comes with unlimited cloud storage for all photos taken on Fire devices

Battery: The battery in this tablet lasts for 12 hours because it's a 4,750-mAh battery, but it can even last the whole day if you use it optimally.

Camera: There is a VGA front facing and a 2MP back facing camera with 720p HD video recording.

Audio: Fire HD 8 has stereo speakers that are customized with Dolby Audio for high quality and rich sounds.

Operating System: Fire OS 5 which has been developed by Google makes browsing through your tablet simple, as it gives it the feel of a magazine.

Kindle Fire HD 10

Price: $229.99 for 16GB, $159.99 for 32GB and $289.99 for 64GB

Color: It comes in 3 colors- Black, Silver Aluminum, White

Screen: It has a 10.1-inch widescreen (1280x800 pixels) HD display, which comes with over a million pixels (149 ppm).

Performance: It comes with Quad-core 1.5 GHz processor, and the RAM is 1 GB.

Storage: It comes with 16GB/32GB/64GB memory, but you can expand the storage to 200GB with the support of a MicroSD card. It has unlimited cloud storage for all photos taken on Fire devices.

Battery: The battery in this tablet lasts for 8 hours because it's a 4,750-mAh battery, but it can even last the whole day if you use it optimally.

Camera: There is 720p HD Front Facing and a 5MP back facing camera with 1080p HD video recording.

Audio: Fire HD 10 has stereo speakers that are customized with Dolby Audio for high quality and rich sounds.

Operating System: Fire OS-5 has been developed by Google makes browsing through your tablet simple, as it gives it the feel of a magazine.

Comparison with other Tablet Devices

There are only a few other tablets in the market that can compete with the Amazon Fire HD Kindle and they are, Samsung's Galaxy S2 Tab and iPad Mini 4.

IPad Mini 4

They are pretty much the same when it comes to comparison in terms of screen and display, except that iPad Mini 4 has a better resolution and pixel density. This is offset by the higher price that comes with iPad Mini; another disadvantage is that Apple does not give you the option for expanding your storage which can be quite troublesome.

Galaxy S2

Galaxy S2 is almost as expensive as the iPad Mini, which is why it offers you with a better resolution and also a better camera. If you are someone that wants a better experience regarding using your tablet as your major electronic device, then you should consider these as important factors because in consideration with the price, Kindle Fire HD gives you a lot of essential functions that a tablet should provide.

Further, the Galaxy s2 has 1.9 GHz processor that enhances its speed and performance; it also has a high storage capacity, and this can be useful if you are looking to store some memory gouging stuff.

Chapter 2:

GETTING STARTED

This chapter will help you out with the basics of using your Kindle. You can start with taking the device out of the box and then just follow the instructions in this chapter so that you can get familiar with your device and start using it.

Controls and Battery

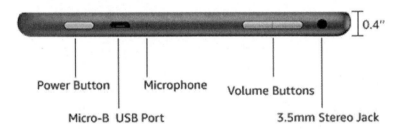

You can find the power button of your Kindle Fire HD at top right corner, it's a silver button, and you can also see the front facing camera, which is in the middle of the top panel of the device. You will also find the volume adjusting buttons on the top left edge of your device; as it's obvious from their name these buttons can be used to change the volume as required.

Start your Device

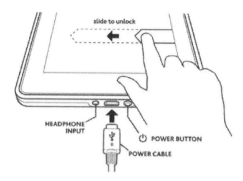

If you want to start your device, then press the power button for a few seconds, if you want to close your device after you are done using it then just click on the power button once. If you want to use your device, just click on the power button and then slide your fingers up from the button panel of your device. Shutting off the device requires you to press and hold the button for a few seconds and then you will have to select the option to shut down or cancel. You will find a headphone jack on the top edge that can be used to plug in your Fire HD headphones and listen to music or watch movies.

Charging for the First Time

The Kindle Fire HD tablet comes slightly charged, but you should start charging it as soon as you take it out of the box. You will find the USB cable and the USB adapter in the box, which you need to connect to a power outlet and then your Kindle Fire HD. You can find the USB port on your device at the bottom, just next to the power button and you are ready to go.

You can check if your device is being charged or not by looking at the battery-shaped icon at the top right. There will be a small lightning shape that will be visible on the battery, which shows that your device is now charging. If you want, you can even use other ways to charge your battery, such as charging directly from your laptop or computer but it'll take more time than a regular charger.

It takes 5-6 hours to charge the tablet completely. Unless you are doing a crazy amount of work, you will be able to use your tablet for 12 hours at an average. You can use your tablet in either portrait or landscape; that depends on you. The screen of your tablet will adjust depending on your preference.

The Kindle Fire HD is a touch-screen tablet, so you will be using your fingers to navigate through everything. Touch screens are simple; you will get used to them as your continue using your device. Just click once if you want to open something, locate the symbol of the app by going to your tablet by sliding your fingers. This will help you to do things like change screens or turn a page while reading a book.

Setup and Registration

As soon as you switch on your tablet, you'll see an introduction that will guide you through the basics about your device and then it will lead you to the registration. It is necessary to register your device if you want to start using it and the device will keep reminding you till you register.

The registration is supposed to connect your device to the Amazon cloud server. It is important for you to register because there are a lot of benefits that come with the device but are dependent upon you registering your device. These advantages include

- Downloading movies,
- Getting Amazon updates
- Using the Amazon streaming service and
- Access to free music

The account that you will use to register is the same one that you must have used to buy your device, so there is no need to create a new account but if you don't have an account for any reason, go ahead and create an Amazon account before you log in.

#1 Step: Switch on the device

So, let's begin by turning on the device; the first thing that you will see is the option to select your language, choose one, and then proceed further.

#2 Step: Connect to WiFi

Next thing you need to do is connect your tablet to a wireless network. The Kindle Fire HD 8 and 10 can only connect to the internet with the help of Wireless networks because they can't be inserted with SIM cards, so you have to select a wireless network.

Your device will scan the area for your nearby networks, those networks that are password protected will have a lock symbol right next to them, and you can't access these networks without a password. Ideally, you should select a network that you are familiar with or that you own, you can select open networks if you trust the source such as networks that are available at restaurants or colleges.

If the wireless network that you want to connect with requires a password, then, click on the network. The tablet's inbuilt keyboard will pop up so that you can type the password.

If you want to add numerical values while typing just click on the option that you see at the bottom left corner. If you want to capitalize then click on the option that is on the bottom left and looks like an upward arrow. You are all done now, just click on connect, and the network will be saved so that your device can connect to it whenever you open it. To put it simply, you don't have to connect to the same network again and again.

#3: Download Software

You have to connect to the Internet if you want to continue with the setup of your device because the tablet needs to download some relevant software to function, this download will begin automatically if you connect to a wireless network. The download will take about 15-20 minutes if you have a good internet connection and might even take longer if it is slow.

#4: Registration

As soon as the download is done, a new screen will appear for registering your device. You'll have to type your email address and password for your Amazon account, and if you don't have an account, then you should click on create new account. Click on continue after that, check that the time zone that has been selected by your tablet is the correct one.

There is a chance that you might see a Deregister option instead of the Register option. The reason for this is you must have received your Kindle Fire HD as a gift. All you have to do is Deregister and then register again.

#5: Transfer Data from old Kindle Device

You also get the option of transferring all your data from previous devices into your new device. If you owned a previous Kindle device, and you want to transfer majority data from there, then you can do so by clicking on the **Choose Backup File** option. You'll be able to see your previous Amazon devices now. All you have to do is click on the device you want to get data from. If you don't want to use the data from your previous device but want to do it all from scratch, just click on **Do Not Restore**.

You will also get the option to import the profiles that you created on your previous devices. These are the profiles that you added to your **Family Library** so that other people in your household can also use the device. Just click on the box next to the profiles you want to import and remember that all the data stored with those profiles will be added to your tablet.

#6: Enable Location

Next, you will see the option to **enable location**; enabling location allows certain social media sites and other applications to use your location. If you want to allow such sites or apps to use your location then click on **Enable**, or you can click on **No Thanks**.

You can now connect your Fire HD tablet to your various social media networks such as Facebook, Goodreads, and Twitter, log into them by clicking on the links to these sites and typing in your Id and password to that site. You can also skip this step and complete it after a while by clicking on continue.

#7: Buy Extended Warranty

You can also buy the extended warranty plan to protect your Kindle Fire HD. This option appears under the "**Protect Your Fire Screen**," and you can select this option if you want to buy such a plan. You don't have to do this right now, but whenever you buy a plan, it will be recorded on the date that your device was shipped and not the date that you purchased the plan. If you want to decline then tap "No Thanks" and if you want to buy, such plans then click on "Purchase."

Now, you will be given a small tutorial on how to use your Kindle Fire HD, click on the orange prompt buttons to get through the tutorial and then click "Exit" to end it. You can also skip the tutorial if you wish by clicking on the "Exit" button before the tutorial starts.

Once the setup is complete, you will be able to see your home screen that you can use to navigate through the various functions that your device can perform. If you used the restore option then your home screen will show the customized preferences that you had on your previous device.

Navigation

Navigation in your Kindle Fire HD is pretty simple; you have to use your home screen to do it. If you ever get lost while using your device or just want to start from the beginning, click on the small circular button at the bottom of your screen; you will be redirected to your home screen.

There are a few basic components of your Home screen that you need to familiarize yourself with to use your tablet efficiently.

Status Bar: At the top of your screen, you will see a bar that displays major information about your device. You will see small symbols here that are essential for your device:

- Battery status
- Local Time
- Wireless network you're connected to
- Notifications from various applications

Search Box: You will see a small box with a magnifying glass just below the status bar, this box can be used to search your device as well as the Internet, and it's a Google prompt button that directs you to Google/Bing if you enter any query.

It can also be used to search the content of your tablet and the content of your Amazon library. You can also search with the help of voice command by clicking on the small microphone icon and then speak whatever you want the device to search. If the voice command wasn't clear, then you will see some suggested options, and you can click on the suggestion that fits your search.

The Fire HD automatically searches the internet first. If you want it to search Amazon instead, then tap the center of the bar right above the search box. If you want to search through the data on your device, then you have to type "My Stuff" on the right side of the bar that is above the search box. You can also do all of this by swiping right or left after you have searched something.

Category Bar: This bar shows you the various categories that you can access on your device; it helps you to navigate through the huge amount of functions that you can perform with your tablet. The bar is right below the search box, and the first option on it is **Recent** and then **Home**, followed by some other options. You can use this bar to access all the data that Amazon gives you access to such as millions of books, movies, apps, games and songs. This bar will help you navigate through all the stuff that you buy from

Amazon and you can even use it to shop for new stuff.

You can swipe to access the various categories, or you can click on the category and the screen will display the entries under that particular category. The screen that will appear when you click on a certain category will show you a magazine style view. You can use that to access your content through the rows of content that you have purchased. You will also see a small part of the screen at the bottom, which shows the content that is recommended for you and on the right side you can see a small box for searching through that category.

You can also see a small "**Library**" option on the far right side of each category; you can click this option to look at all the content that you own on a single screen and also to find the content that you are looking for. You will be able to see two options when you click on "Library". One is the "**All Option**" that you can use to find the content that is stored in your Amazon cloud. This is the content that you safely store through online servers of Amazon. The other option is "**Downloaded**" which shows the content you downloaded and stored in your device. You will see a small checkbox along with the icon of your content, a tick on this box means that you have downloaded that content and it is stored on your device.

You can see a sort icon under the Library option on the far top right. Use this option to manage your content and sort it into a certain way that you prefer. It will only change the order in which the content appears and make it more systematic, depending on the option that you pick.

You will also see the option of "**Store**" on the right side of each category under the Category bar. The option looks like a small shopping cart and it can be used to access the Amazon online stores.

Clicking on the store option will take you to the Amazon store where you will see various recommendations, sub-categories and popular choices to sort from in order to find and buy the content that you are looking for. If you want to shop for all the categories together by using the Amazon store, then go back on the home screen and click on the Store option in the category bar instead.

You can also access the sidebar Menu in your category; when you click on the library or sort option, you will be able to see the sidebar option on the far left side at the top. You can use this sidebar option to access the library even more easily and it'll make it simpler to navigate through your content. It helps you to find content on the basis of things like popular, favorites and most recent.

New Items: This is the section of your home screen that shows the new content that you can access on your Fire HD tablet. These are random items that you must have downloaded recently and the whole point of this section is to make it easier for you to access stuff that you downloaded recently. It also helps in keeping track of what you downloaded or bought.

This section can be quite annoying at times, and if you don't want to see a clutter of new items that you bought you can remove whichever item you want by simply pressing and holding on that item. You will see an option that says **"Remove from Home"** that will remove it from your home screen but it will still stay in the device or you can click on the option that says, **"Remove from Device"** and it will delete it from your tablet. If you do delete something from your device that does not mean that you have removed it entirely because it will still be stored in your Amazon account so you can download it again from there whenever you want.

App Grid: Apps are software applications that help you to perform certain tasks and activities; they are meant to enhance the experience of your Fire HD tablet. You can view all the applications that you have in the bottom part of your home screen, if you want to open an App then just click on it. If you want to uninstall an app then press and hold till a little checkbox appears then tap the uninstall option that you can now see on your screen. There are some apps cannot be uninstalled since they are pre-installed and are integral to the functioning of the device.

You can change the position of apps by pressing and holding an app then dragging it around, you can arrange the apps in whatever manner you prefer and you can even arrange them in different folders. You can make a folder by dragging an app and combining it with another app, this will automatically create a folder. You can change the name of the folder by clicking on the combined app symbol then using the keyboard type the name of the folder. Click on the yellow checkbox symbol on the keyboard to save the folder name and close the folder.

Navigation Bar: This is the black bar that appears at the bottom of your screen and can be used to change between menu bars.

There are three different options that you can use to go between menus. The left one, which is in the shape of arrow keys, can be used to go back to the previous menu, and it's just like the back option that you see on your browser. You can also use this option to close the on-screen keyboard.

The middle circle can be used to go to your home screen, tap it a couple of times whenever you want to go back to your home screen. It is also important to not leave any applications running since it might slow down the processor of your tablet. So, after you are done using an application, go to the home screen and click on the far right option which looks like a square. You will now be able to see all the open applications and close them.

If you can't see the navigation bar then it is probably because you are in full screen mode and you can exit this mode by clicking once in the middle of the screen.

Content Storage and Access

Content is stored in your Fire HD tablet with the help of the internal memory as well as external memory. As soon as you buy something from the Amazon store it is stored in the cloud and if you want to download it to your device then it is stored in your internal memory as long as there is space.

Micro SD Card Slot

You can store a lot of stuff that you want in an external MicroSD card; there is a slot for inserting the external card that you can find on the top right edge when you hold the device down flat.

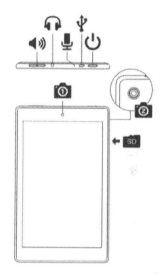

You can take off the slot cover and move it to the side so that you can see the slot, then insert the memory card gently with the top notch facing upward and make sure it is in a position that it can fit the slot. There are only a few cards that are compatible with this device; you can find this list on the Amazon website. After you are done inserting the memory card, remember to carefully close the slot again.

Content Storage is closely related to the cloud; the cloud is just an internet server which holds all the information that you want to store in it. There are certain memory restrictions on the amount of content that you can store on it which is why you should only store those things on the cloud that are really important for you. You can access the things that you save on cloud from any of the devices that you own.

Amazon Cloud

The Amazon Cloud comes pre-installed into your Fire HD tablet. The cloud is important for this tablet because there are certain memory restrictions that it has and to store certain things with the help of the cloud opens up more space for the user. The best part about the Amazon Cloud is that it is

unlimited and you can store all the content that you want there as long as the content has been bought from Amazon stores.

Whenever you buy something from Amazon, you have the option of downloading it to your device. If you want to free up some space you can easily delete whatever you don't want knowing that there is a copy of the same thing that has been stored in the Amazon cloud. So, whenever you need it you can download the content back to your device without paying for it again. If you want to access the cloud and download content onto your device, just click on the category that the content belongs to, then go to library and just tap the item once to download it again. If there is a tick in the checkbox next to the icon it means that the item has already been downloaded to your device.

Amazon Cloud Drive

The Amazon Cloud Drive is a paid product and the benefit that it gives you over the Amazon Cloud is that you can even store non-Amazon bought products on it. You can store any content that you want, be it your personal photos, videos or even movies that you didn't buy from the Amazon store.

Chapter 3:

SETTINGS AND CUSTOMIZATION

The Fire HD tablet comes with already preset settings that have been customized to provide you with the best experience. There are settings that you might want to change to fit your needs and hence, you can customize the whole device so that it's easier for you to handle.

The Menu

There are two kinds of menus that are available; you can use both of these menus to change your settings.

Quick Settings Menu

This is the menu where you can find settings that you will most likely use; the whole point of this menu is to make your life easier so that you don't have to open the settings menu for every little thing.

You can find this menu by swiping down from the top edge of your screen, it's hidden in a way but it's easy to access as all you have do is swipe down. You will see various settings in this menu that you will be likely to use on a daily basis. You can hide this menu again by swiping it upwards or you can simply press the back arrow button at the bottom navigation bar. This back arrow button will also be used if you go into a sub-settings menu option.

Brightness: It's the slider at the top with the sun icon. Brightness is the amount of background light that you need at any point of time while using your device. You can adjust the brightness by using the slider, sliding towards right is increasing and vice-versa.

Wireless Network: You can connect to Wi-Fi networks with the help of this, your tablet will automatically connect to the wireless network that you have saved. If you want to disable wireless networks then just click on the network symbol once.

Airplane Mode: You can use this option to turn off all the networks your tablet is connected to. Your tablet is only connected to Wi-Fi networks most of the time; you can use this option to close your wireless networks when you are not in need of them.

Bluetooth: This option can be used to make your device discoverable by other Bluetooth devices. Just click on the Bluetooth symbol and then switch icon so that you can connect to items that use Bluetooth such as microphones and speakers.

Do Not Disturb: This option can be used to turn off all sounds and notifications so that you are not disturbed while you are doing something important.

Firefly: The Firefly app can be opened with the help of this and then you can use the app to scan products. Scanning products helps you to find them online in order to get more information about them or even to buy them. It can also be used to identify audio in order to tell you the name of the song, movie or TV Show that you are watching.

Help: It connects you to the various online Amazon help resources that are available and provides you with information on how to connect to the Amazon customer service.

Auto-Rotate: You can use this option to lock the device so that your screen does not rotate when you rotate your device or you can enable the option if you want.

Settings: You can use this option to go to the settings menu where you can find a huge list of settings which will help you to customize your tablet in detail. The long settings menu can also be accessed by clicking on the application that is available in the App grid.

The Settings Menu

There are various settings that are available under this menu and you can use it to customize or change almost anything in your device. There is a huge list of options that are available as you go to the settings menu and each menu has sub-menus.

Wireless: This is the same as the wireless menu that is there in the Quick Settings Menu. It can be used to connect and disconnect from wireless networks.

Storage: You can use this menu to delete content from storage; you can also use it to check the amount of space that is available in your internal and external storage.

Further, you can browse through the things that you have stored in your internal and external storage. You can even transfer content to your external storage from internal storage by clicking on items in the internal storage and checking if there is an option to move them to external storage.

Power: There are various options that are available under this menu to conserve power. You have options such as Automatic Smart Suspend and it simply disconnects your device from all wireless networks when you are not using it. You can even check what is eating up most of your battery and then conserve your battery life accordingly.

Apps and Games: You can use this menu to browse through your apps and customize them as you want. You can see which apps are running, see what apps are there on your device, change the notification settings of apps or even uninstall apps. You can deal with the way the app is stored in your device and how it interacts with your device in terms of permissions.

Display: You can deal with the brightness of the display or the amount of time it takes before your screen goes to sleep. To put it simply, it deals with the functions that are related to your screen. You can even use this menu to set wallpaper, which is the background that you can see at your home screen. Display mirroring is another option that you can use to connect your device to another screen, such as that of your television or your laptop.

Device Options: You can use this option to check the basic settings of your device and learn about the specifications of your device. You can even enable things like Find Your Device so that you can find your device if it is stolen. There are also options like restore to Factory Defaults, which you can use if you want to wipe off all the data from your device and set it up again from scratch.

My Account: You can use this option to see what accounts your device is connected to with respect to your email address. It lets you deal with your Amazon account through this menu. You can manage all the accounts that you have logged into on various apps and websites with the help of this menu. It further allows you to change their settings and register or deregister yourself if you want.

Profiles and Family Library: This option helps you to add your family to your device and they can all have different profiles that are customized according to their preferences. You can have up to 2 adults and 4 children profiles on your tablet, these profiles can be used to make your tablet into a family device that can take care of everyone's needs.

Parental Controls: You can setup parental control so that you can control what your kids see by selecting this option and then again clicking this option in the sub-menu. You will now be asked to type in a password that you will have to type if you want to visit certain websites; this password can be anything that your kids can't figure out. Finally, click on "Confirm" and then tap "Finish".

This would bring you to a menu where you can select the items you want under parental control; all the items you select will now need a password in order to be accessed. You can review Parental Control later by using this menu only and retyping your password.

Security: In this menu you can set a password for your device, which would make it more secure, and people will only be able to access it if they have the password. You have various kinds of security codes that you can set; you can set a normal password, a PIN or even a pattern. You will be asked to enter this security code every time you open your tablet and slide towards the right so make sure that it is something easy to remember. If you want you can even write it down on a piece of paper but make sure you keep it in a secure location.

Sound and Notifications: You can deal with the settings in relation to sound, like adjusting your speaker volume or setting the volume for different things such as notifications and calls. You can also set what apps you want to receive notifications from such as if you want the calendar app to give you a notification about your next appointment.

Keyboard and Language: You can determine what language you want to type under this menu by clicking on the Language submenu and selecting your preferred language from the list.

Further, you can use the various submenus to customize your keyboard so that it's easier for you to type. If you want to customize then click on the option of "Fire Keyboard" and then select one of the options. You will see various options such as auto-capitalization, auto-correct (automatically corrects if your spell a word incorrectly) and you can even determine if you want to see suggestions of words while you're typing or not.

You can change the settings for keyboard sounds (whether you want them or not) and you can enable things like trace typing.

Sync Device: This is the menu that you can use to check your connection with the Amazon Cloud and to make sure that all the content that you have purchased has been saved by the Amazon cloud. Also, you can check if your device is updated with the latest items of your purchase.

Help: This is similar to the Help option that is available under the Quick Settings Menu.

Accessibility: There are various sub-menus under this that help you to enhance your experience while you're working on your device. You can change the voice-to-text feature to determine if your voice should be read slower or faster. There are other options that you can go through and change the settings depending on your needs.

Legal and Compliance: There are no user-based changes that you can make under this menu and it's pretty redundant.

Using the Keyboard

The Kindle Fire HD tablet has a typical keyboard that you might see in any smart device. If you want to write something in any space, then all you need to do is click in the text box and the on-screen keyboard will pop up by itself. If you want to remove the keyboard from the screen then click on the down arrow in the navigation bar at the bottom of your screen.

You can get **numbers** on your keyboard by clicking on the numbers and symbols icon at the bottom left of your keyboard. You can **delete** things by clicking on the Delete button at the right side of the keyboard. You can **switch to another language** by pressing and holding the space button. You can **capitalize** or lock capitalization by using the shift key at the left side, click on the shift key once if you want just one capital letter or click on it twice to lock it so that you only type in capitals.

Click on the spacebar twice to get a period and then automatically start a new sentence. The period key can also be used to bring up new punctuations if you press it for a few seconds.

When you are on the numbers and symbols menu of the keyboard and you want to **add symbols**, you should click on the shift key. The shift key will show you other symbols such as foreign currency, percentage, etc. You will see a small edit tool whenever you tap on an empty area near the text box after you are done typing. You have to then drag this small edit tool to the place in the text where you want to edit and then just tap again outside when you are finished editing.

You can **cut, copy or paste** by simply pressing and holding on a certain part of the text that you want to use these functions on. Now, you will see that part of the text as highlighted and you will also see two small arrows on either side of the text; you can drag to cover more text under the highlight. You will then see the cut or copy option and you paste by pressing and holding at the area where you want to paste the text.

Trace Typing with Fire HD

Trace typing is pretty simple; you will be swiping your fingers over the letters. You will have to press the letters that you want to type for just a little longer so that the keyboard can read what letters you want to insert.

You can enable Trace typing from the Keyboard and Languages menu in Settings. Trace typing is pretty simple and you have to be just a little strategic; swipe your way across the letters of the word you want inserted. You have to lift your finger as soon as you reach the last letter of the world you wanted to insert.

To put it simply, you don't have to take your finger away from the screen once you start swiping it. The software detects all the possible words that you could have meant and selects the one that is appropriate. So, once you select an alphabet, continue to swipe to the next alphabet all the while touching the alphabets in the middle.

Trace typing can be slightly difficult but it saves a ton of time and it might not be absolutely accurate. So, if you are someone who is comfortable with it then you should definitely use it.

Chapter 4:

USING INTERNET ON YOUR DEVICE

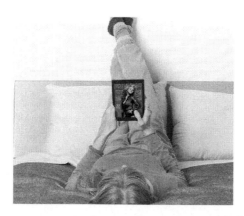

You must have connected to the Internet while you were registering and you can see the Wi-Fi connectivity with the help of the Quick Settings Menu. Click on the Wireless symbol if you want to connect, disconnect or change networks.

Setup Email, Calendar, and Contacts

Email

Fire HD's email app allows you to connect with almost every major email service such as Gmail or Yahoo. You have to follow the steps mentioned and add your account from these sites in a similar manner. You can check your **inbox** by clicking on the option in the sidebar menu.

Steps to setup email

#1: Click on the **email app** that you can find in the apps grid

#2: Click on the "**Add Account**" option

#3: You will be asked to type the email and password of your account, type and then click **accept.**

This will set up your email account and you will this message.

Now your tablet will now login and sync with your email. Next you will see a small tutorial on how to use your email; the tutorial is a little long but you should go through it. Please remember, it is advisable to add your email account that is connected with Amazon account first. You can add other email accounts later.

PoP3, IMAP or Microsoft Exchange?

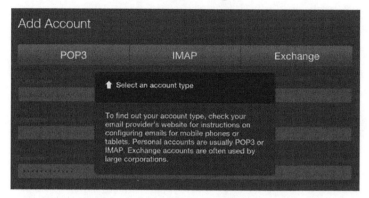

For some email service providers you will see the option to store your email as a POP3, IMAP or Microsoft exchange account. POP3 allows you to download all the emails to your device so that you can view them and IMAP leaves them on the server of your email provider. SO, you can access it on your tablet or any other device by just using the Internet. You can use Microsoft Exchange accounts to setup email accounts that are related to your workplace. Select the type of account you want and then follow the app to setup your email. The basics of how to use email are similar and you can use the email app as you would on your laptop or phone.

Change Email Settings

You can change the settings of your email app and accounts by sliding your finger from the left so that you can see the sidebar menu. You will have to scroll a little to see the settings menu which you can use to add new accounts, change settings of certain accounts and even delete accounts. If you delete an account then remember that the settings and contacts of that account will be deleted along with it. Also, all the information that you had on your tablet from that account will also be removed.

You can make various changes to the accounts and set up preferences. You can name your accounts so that you can differentiate between them; you can even determine if you want daily notifications. You can also get notifications as soon as you receive a mail and you can set up how many emails should the device store in its internal memory.

Other than that, the usual things such as font, signatures and other things that are common to emails can also be setup by using this menu. Using the email app is pretty simple; you can check your inbox and other folders from the side-menu in the app that you can get by swiping from the left. You can reply, forward or reply all to people by simply going to the email and clicking on the reply or forward option. You can compose emails by clicking on the small blue pencil icon at the lower right corner. You will have to save the contact person if you don't already have the email address of the person you're sending the mail to. You can do this by clicking on the small plus icon.

You can attach things by clicking on the small attachment folder and download things by clicking on the attachments and selecting the download option. You can view the downloaded content in the Downloads app in the app grid.

Calendar

You can find the Calendar app in the apps grid and it works like any other calendar app that you have ever seen. It syncs automatically with your email accounts so that you don't have to do anything at all. It will also give you notifications if you have enabled them in the settings but notifications are enabled automatically on your tablet so unless you changed the settings you don't have to do anything at all.

Contacts

Your tablet automatically syncs with your email accounts and gets your contacts from there. If you want to view, add, edit or delete your contacts then you have to use the contacts app that you can find in the Apps grid.

You can get contacts or send them from other apps as well by using the menu icon with the three vertical dots in the top of the right corner. Tap the option that you wish in order to import or export contacts or tap settings to change your Contact options.

Shopping on Fire

You can shop on the Amazon app by going to different categories under the category tab and selecting the shop option. You can also do this by clicking on the Amazon shopping app in the apps grid.

Setup 1-Click Payment

You have to setup one click payment if you want to shop on the Amazon site for anything; you can do this by entering the details about your credit card.

- You have to go to the "**My Account**" option
- Click on Amazon Account Settings
- Click on Payment options.

You can edit your one click payment option by going to your Amazon account and clicking on edit.

Shopping category wise is as explained before and it's pretty much like shopping on the Amazon site. If you open a store you will be able to download whatever you want with the help of your one click payment. You can also buy things later by adding them to your wishlist. You can find the "Add To Wishlist" option just below the product display and you can access your wishlist by sliding from left to right and engaging the sidebar menu.

Your tablet also comes with a one-month free subscription to **Amazon Prime** that you can sign up for whenever you want. You can get a lot of benefits such as access to free eBooks and movies as a Prime member. Further, you get two day free shipping on all your orders.

Using the Browser

The Amazon Silk browser that comes pre-installed with your tablet. You can access the Silk browser by clicking on the Silk app icon in the apps grid.

Basic Functions

It's pretty easy to use, just type the name of the website that you want to visit or that of your search in the search box at the top. In addition, something that has been changed is that instead of the back button in the top menu you will have to use the back button in the navigation bar. Silk also combines the main text box for websites with search function, so as you input any search you will be redirected to Bing search engine results for your query. You can also change to Google search by going in the settings.

You can open a new tab by clicking on the plus sign at the top menu and you can open links without changing the page by pressing and holding on a link and then selecting "Open" in New Tab option. You can go back to the start screen by closing all the tabs, which you can do by clicking on the small x that you can see with the name of each tab.

You will be able to add **bookmarks** by clicking on the ribbon icon in the top menu and you can visit or edit your bookmarks by sliding from left to right so that you can see the sidebar menu. You can use the **sidebar** for various other options, which includes seeing your history and deleting it by clicking on the trash can icon on the top right corner of the History menu.

Customizing your Silk Settings

You have the option of personalizing your browser by clicking on the settings menu and changing the browser to fit your preferences. These preferences include things like clearing cache, managing cookies and changing your pop-ups setting.

There are two different versions of each site that you can access if you want; the first one is the Mobile Version and the Desktop version. You can switch between these two by clicking on the menu option in the far right corner of the menu tabs at the top. Kindle Fire HD is a tablet so it will probably be able to handle most of the Desktop versions of sites but there are some sites that don't have a mobile version at all.

Advanced Functions

You can enlarge the page if you want by double tapping the page to enlarge it and then double tapping it again to reduce it. This acts like magnification and if you are not able to read the content of the page or just prefer the content to be displayed at a certain size you can do this. The other method is known as pinching, you will simply have to place any two fingers on the screen a little apart and pinch them together in order to enlarge or reduce the size of the page.

You can share the link for any website by clicking on the menu icon with three vertical dots in the search bar and then clicking on share. You will see various options to share the website with your contacts like email or messaging apps.

The default search engine that Silk uses is Bing but you can change that to Google by making use of the sidebar menu. Click on "Settings" and then tap on "Search Engine" to change your default search engine to whatever your preference is.

Chapter 5:

ALL ABOUT APPS

Apps or applications are small software programs that compliment any device so that it can perform various specific tasks. There are apps for just about everything these days and if you want to use your tablet to perform any specific task or feature then you can search for an app.

There are certain pre-installed apps that come with your device such as the Silk browser and almost every task on a tablet is performed with the help of applications. Now, you can find any apps that you want with the help of the Amazon App Store that stores and collects all applications so that you can download them.

There are certain apps that have already been explained and almost every app that is there on your device has certain functions such as the Firefly app that you can use to scan items and search for them on the Internet.

Downloading Apps

To download apps

- Go the apps tab under the Category bar
- Click on Store

Amazon has started a new **Amazon Underground** program under which you can download certain apps that qualify for this program and use them for free without any in-app purchases or even subscriptions. You can find the apps that qualify for Amazon Underground in the Amazon Apps Store in the Recommended For You column.

You can look for apps that are available under this program also through the library option under each category and all the apps that carry a small Actually Free banner qualify for it.

If you are not able to find any underground apps then maybe it's because you haven't turned on the **Collect App Usage Data** option under Apps and Games in Settings.

Search for Apps

You can search for apps by using the search box or sorting them by category through the sidebar menu that you can get by sliding from left to right. You can tap on the icon of the app to read more about the app and to look at general reviews of the app.

Therefore, just search and find whatever app you want then click on the app, there are some apps for which you would have to pay with the one-click pay option and there are certain apps which are absolutely free but some free apps also have in-app purchases such as Netflix.

Amazon Coins

You might even see some Amazon coins that you can use to buy apps; this is virtual currency that has been made available by Amazon to purchase apps. You get one Amazon coin when you register; if you want more coins then you have to go to the sidebar menu and click on Amazon coins.

You should verify apps before you download them, just make sure that the app is authentic and the developer isn't a fake. Apps bought are non-refundable so be absolutely sure before you buy an app.

Buying Apps

To download an app click on the price button that can be found near the description. If the app is free it will still be registered as a payment of zero under your one-click payment method. The one-click payment mode will now be activated and the price will now change to Get App; the get app button will automatically start the download.

You can check the status of downloading through the menu at the top. After the download is complete, you can click on Open through the notifications tab or you can find the app later under the Apps Grid. If you can't find the app there then look for it under the Apps tab in the Category Bar.

You can even buy apps from your laptop or PC by using the **Amazon Apps Store** website which will directly link your Amazon account to your Fire HD tablet. It sends the download directly to your device and the download will start as soon you connect your tablet to the Internet.

Uninstalling Apps

You can uninstall apps by going to the Apps category in the Category bar then going to library and clicking on the small menu tab next to the app. Finally, select the option that says '**delete from device**'. Deleting apps regularly is a good thing because storage on your device is limited but you can even buy a Micro SD card so that you don't have such problems.

If you uninstall a paid app from your device, it is still available on your Amazon cloud. You can download it back by going to the navigation bar and selecting Apps then clicking on the orange arrow to download it back.

Force Closing Apps

If an app stops working or if you simply want to stop the functioning of an app you can Force Close it. You can do this by

- Going to the Settings Menu
- Clicking on Apps and Games
- Click on manage all applications.

You will now see a list of all downloaded and installed applications that are currently on your device. Click on the icon of the app that you want to Force Close and then click on the **Force Close** option to stop it from functioning. This option can be helpful if your app hangs up.

Installing 3rd Party Apps

There are certain apps that you will not be able to find in the Amazon apps store; these are apps that you can only find on the Android Play Store. It can be complex to download such apps that are not supported by Amazon and some of these apps won't run on your Fire tablet at all. Although, you can always try because you can't really know which apps work with your tablet and which don't.

All you have to do is

- Go the **Settings Menu** and then tap '**Security**'
- Go to the option for **Apps from Unknown Sources**

You have to enable it so that the switch icon is now orange. This means that you have given permission to your device so that it can download apps that are not verified by Amazon and are third party apps.

Downloading 3rd Party Apps

You can find various App Stores online from where you can download the setup of various Android applications and then hope that they run on your device. But first you need to download the software of these applications that is known as **.APK files**.

First, try the Silk browser's sidebar menu and click on the Downloads button, find the .APK extension file and click on it. This will start the download and if it doesn't then try clicking on Notifications.

Notifications is the second way to download these apps, you can do this by sliding down the Quick Settings Menu and if you see a notification with the name of the app, click on it and see if it starts downloading.

The last option is to download application ES File Explore or File Expert. Navigate to find the Downloads option in your internal storage and click on the .APK file to install it. The installation process after this is similar to the apps that you download from the Amazon store.

Chapter 6:

READINGS BOOKS AND NEWSSTAND ITEMS

Nobody does it better than Amazon when it comes to books; Amazon has the biggest collection of books anywhere and it's easy to use their book library. The Kindle Fire HD is the perfect device that you can have to buy and read books.

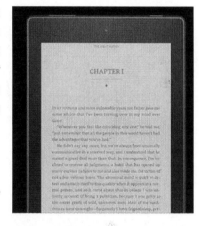

Buy Books from Amazon

- Go to the **Books** tab under the Category Bar
- Click on "**Shop**" if you want to buy books from the Amazon bookstore.

There are various schemes that Amazon has such as **Kindle Unlimited** that require you to pay a monthly subscription in order to have free access to a huge variety of books.

You will see a lot of options such as Best Sellers and Recommended for you that you can make use of to browse through the books and select the one you want. You can find additional categories to advance your search by sliding from left to right and using the sidebar menu. You can typically search the store by using the search box at the top.

You simply have to click on a book in order to read its description and you can also read the user reviews by other Amazon account shoppers. There is a Download Sample button that you can click on and it downloads a small sample of the book to your device; you will have to tap on Read Now to go through the sample. You can also add books to your Wishlist by clicking on the 'More' option and you can view your Wishlist by using the sidebar menu.

To Buy a Book

- Click on the buy button that is near the description
- Then your one-click payment mode will be charged.

The button will now change to download; if you are downloading a free book then it will be charged as zero. When the downloading is done, the button will read as 'Read Now'.

You can also buy an eBook from Amazon website on your pc or laptop and send it your kindle. It will automatically be downloaded when you connect to the internet and if that doesn't happen go the Settings and click on Sync Device.

Reading Books on Fire HD

You can go to your Books library to read the books that you purchased by clicking on Books in the category bar. All the newly purchased books will have a small cover that says new on them.

The cover will also show you a number that indicates the percentage of that book you have read so far; this is for when you are in the middle of reading a book. Tap on the book and wait for it to open, you can swipe left or right to navigate through the pages.

If you open a book then the navigation bar will disappear since your tablet is now in full page mode. You have to just click once in the center of the screen to get the navigation bar back and you will also see a slider that shows where you are in that book; you can use the slider to jump to a certain part of the book. If you now swipe left or right, you will see a table of contents with the name of each chapter that you can click if you want to jump to the starting of a certain chapter. If you want to go back to the full screen mode, tap the page again.

Using Word Runner

There is also the option of Word Runner that you can use; it's an option that helps you to read faster by displaying words one at a time at a speed of your choice. If you want to enable this option then

- Tap the menu icon with the three verticals dots,
- Click on **word runner** and then the forward arrow to start it.

Just press and hold the screen if you want a break and you will also see a speed bar that you can use to deal with the speed.

Download or Delete a Book

Go to the Library option under the Books tab if you want to delete or download a book. If you want to download a book, then tap "All" and click on the book's icon to download it to your device from the cloud. Deleting a book is also simple, click on Downloaded and then press the book for a couple of seconds till a trashcan icon appears. Clicking on it will remove the book from your tablet but it will stay be available for download through the cloud.

You can deal with books storage by downloading the eBook that you want to read from the cloud to your device and deleting those that you don't need. You should always keep those books that you plan to read, on your device instead of the cloud because you can only access the cloud with a wireless network. This may be difficult to find if you're outside of your house or at a park.

Reading Accessibility Feature

You can use the reading toolbar to customize your reading experience so that you are comfortable with the way that you are reading. To access the toolbar, click on the screen while reading any book and you will see it at the top- it has various options to enhance your experience.

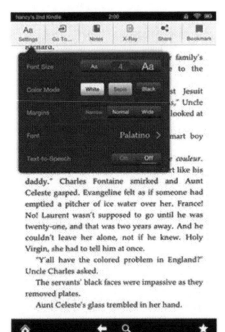

You can click on "Aa" option to change the background, text color, size, font and the spacing between words. You can even go to additional settings by clicking on the menu symbol which has three vertical dots on it. You will see various options that will help you to change the way you were reading to better fit your needs.

Text-to-Speech: This button will let your tablet read the book to you; it's only available for those books that have Text-to-Speech enabled. So, check if the book you are buying has this option while you are buying it by going through the description.

X-Ray: It's a tool that will give you additional information about the author or specific parts of the book. It can be beneficial for your book club or even students. If you enable X-Ray then you will be able to see the full list of such passages that have information and facts related to them.

Share: You can copy and paste parts of a book on your social media sites or send them to your friends.

Bookmark: You just have to click on this option and tap the upper right corner of the page that you're reading to create a bookmark. So, whenever you open the book again this is the page that you'll start from. If you click on the option then you will be able to see the bookmark option on the reading toolbar and it may automatically be there as well so that you don't have to enable it.

Notes and Highlighting: You just have to tap the part of the book that you want to highlight by dragging your finger through the section and adjusting the highlighted part with the help of arrows. You will then get various options to add notes, share or highlight; you can look at your notes or highlighted section by clicking on the Notes option that is available on the Reading Toolbar.

You can also see parts of the book that have been highlighted by other people under the "**Popular Highlights**" option. This can be found by swiping downward to display the Quick Settings Menu, going to Apps and Games, then the submenu Amazon Application Settings, followed by Reader Settings and you will the option of Popular Highlights.

Word Wise: You can use this option to get slight hints about words that you are reading, you can set the parameter to determine if easy or difficult words should be shown under Word Wise.

Dictionary: Simply tap on a word and hold for a few seconds to bring up a dictionary meaning of that word, you can then click on Full Definition to see the complete definition or even search the web for the word. You also get the option of translating that word to your language by simply inputting the name of your language. The language option is at the corner of the definition box.

Goodreads: Goodreads is now owned by Amazon so you can directly sync your book reading with this website, so that when you purchase or start reading a book it will automatically be posted to your Goodreads account.

To go to Goodreads, click on the Books tab under the Category Bar, tap Library and you will see the Goodreads option at the top of your screen. You just need your login id and password to get access to the account and to sync it your Amazon reading.

Downloading Free eBooks

You can use various third party websites to get access to free eBooks; you just have to simply search using your Silk browser for the free book. You can even use Amazon services such as Amazon classics which are books that are old and whose copyright has expired so you can now read them for free. You just have to type free popular classics or something like that into your search box while shopping.

You can also use the Kindle Select 25 that is the top 25 books that have been made free by their author to increase their demand. These books change every week and you can access this by going to the sidebar menu.

If you use a third party website such as Internet Archive or Open Library, you would have to download the book with the help of your browser or PC and download the kindle version. If you use a laptop, you would then have to transfer it your kindle. Then you can access these books as they appear in the Library under the Books tab.

Borrowing and Lending Books on Amazon

You can borrow books with the help of Amazon prime membership and it simply means that you have to pay a small charge to borrow a book. It is limited to borrowing only one book per month from Amazon but you wouldn't have any due dates.

You have to go the Books Store and then swipe left to right to see the sidebar option, and then select the Kindle Owner Lending Library. This will show you the books that you can borrow from

Amazon for free. Click on the book to read the description, click on Borrow for Free if you want to read the book and then the book will be downloaded to your device. You can read the book just like you would a book you paid for; you can even add notes and highlights to it.

You can simply return a book by borrowing another one and while doing this; it will ask you to return the previous book that you have borrowed. There are other options such as going to the home screen of your Silk browser and clicking on Manage Your Fire from the menu that would drop down once you click on my Your Account option. You will see Actions button next to the titles that you want to return, click on them and follow the instructions.

Newsstand Items: Buying and Reading

You can use your tablet to subscribe to newspapers or magazines so that you can read them on a daily basis.

- Go to the Newsstand Tab under the Category Bar

- Go to store

- Browse through the items and select the one you want

- Click on Subscribe Now or Try Free for 30 Days and you will be able to read the daily or monthly editions with the help of your one-click payment option.

There are certain newsstand items that need a lot of features and have separate apps that you can get from the App store and then deal with subscription by using in-app purchases.

You can view the Newsstand items you have bought by going to the Library option under the Newsstand tab. You will only see the current issue of your items and to see the previous issues just click on the name of the title under the 'All' tab of the library.

Chapter 7:

LISTENING TO MUSIC AND MANAGING YOUR MUSIC FILES

Your Fire tablet is the perfect device to listen to music; it has great speakers and holding the tablet in any position does not interfere with the sound quality at all.

Buying Music

If you want to buy music from Amazon then

- Click on the Music tab in the category bar
- Go to Store.

There are millions of songs in the Amazon store that you can go through and download the ones that you want.

You can find music that is recommended for you based on your previous purchases by clicking on the Store icon at the top. If you want to search through the store on the basis of genres, categories or artists you can use the tabs that are available just above the Store screen.

If you want to learn more about a certain item then just click on the thumbnail to expand the selection. You can also listen to a sample of the song by clicking on the circled number next to the item. You can use the search box at the top to look for any song, album or artist.

Buying an item is also simple, just click the price button which will then change to Buy Now; this is similar to any other Amazon store as your one-click payment method is activated. If the song is free then zero dollars will be charged to your one-click payment method. Click on "Buy Now", this will store your purchase in the Amazon cloud so that you can access it later. A small pop-up will appear now asking you if you want to listen to the song in your Music Library or continue to shop for more songs.

If you are a Prime member then you can use the sidebar menu to access millions of free songs, albums and playlists; just swipe left to right to show the sidebar menu. You will find all the free songs that you are entitled to under this menu; you just have to click on the plus icon next to any song in order to add it your Amazon cloud. There are playlists that are also available for your selection; you can add the whole playlist by clicking on the menu icon with three vertical dots which will lead to a pop-up window. You can also go ahead and select a single song from the playlist by clicking on the Add button next to it.

Listening to your Music

If you want to listen to Music then

- Tap the Music tab from the Category Bar
- Click on Library to go through all the music that you have bought.

If you want to sort through your music or if you want to view your recent activity then swipe from left to right to display the sidebar menu. You can use it to find the music that is stored in the cloud and the music that you have stored offline.

Just tap any item to open it and it will automatically start playing. You can adjust the volume, stop and replay or skip songs by using the appropriate buttons that you can see when you open an item.

Song Lyrics

There is also a song lyrics feature. This feature enables you to see the lyrics while listening to the song, along with facts about the song and the artists. There are a lot of songs that don't come with this feature so don't be alarmed if you don't see the lyrics.

There is an app that you can use to stream music that is stored in your Amazon Cloud library; you can also download the music and listen offline. Although, it is better to listen to music from your Amazon Cloud because there is only a certain amount of space on your device and music can take a lot of that space. It only takes a little more battery life to listen to music that is stored on the cloud but it also saves a lot of space.

The app can be used by clicking on the Music tab from the Category Bar and then clicking on Library. You will automatically see the songs that are stored on your cloud but if you see, the songs that you have downloaded to your device then swipe from left to right in order to display the sidebar menu and then click on Offline Library.

Similarly, if you want to see the songs that are stored on your device then open the sidebar menu and click on Offline Library. You can download songs from the cloud to your device by selecting a song while in the Cloud Library in your music app, clicking on the menu button with three vertical dots and then selecting download.

You can remove a song from your device by using the same method and then clicking on Remove from Device in the popup menu.

Buying and Listening to Audiobooks

There is a separate Audiobook tab under the Category Bar that you can use to access the Audiobook store and it functions similarly to the Books Store that has been explained previously. You can also use the Library button to look through the Audiobooks that you have purchased and listen to them. The Audiobooks function similarly as music and can be stored on the cloud or downloaded to the device.

If you click on an Audiobook in order to listen to it then you will be able to see a panel that you can use to control the speed, add bookmarks, pause, and adjust the volume. You can also use the sleep function so that your Fire can read the book for a certain amount of time which is an estimate in terms of the amount of time it will take for you to fall asleep.

Managing your Music Library

Creating Playlists

If you want to create a playlist of your favorite songs, and then just go to any song, click on the small menu icon with three vertical dots that is next to it, and then from the popup menu select Add to Playlist. You can add the song to an existing playlist by clicking on the name of that list or you can create a new one by clicking on the plus icon which means Create New Playlist. You'll have to name the playlist and then click on Save.

You can view your playlists by clicking on the Playlist button on the far left of the Menu Bar which you can see at the top. You can also remove songs from a playlist by clicking on the menu bar and then on Remove from Playlist.

You will also see some Playlists that you can buy for free if you are a Prime member. These are pre-made playlists by Amazon for your convenience and you can download them from the Playlist tab.

Transferring to and from the Amazon Cloud Drive

With Amazon cloud you get the option of importing your personal music to your Amazon Cloud so that you can listen to the music that you already have on all your Amazon devices.

You can do this by going the **Amazon Music Library** on the Amazon website from your laptop. You have to scroll down the sidebar menu on this page and click on Upload Your Music. You will then have to install the Amazon music app; this app will go through all the music that you have stored on your device as well as services such as iTunes. You can choose which songs you want to upload to the drive or you can simply click Upload All.

Now, you can access all the uploaded songs on your Fire Tablet with the help of the Amazon Cloud.

Chapter 8:

WATCHING MOVIES

Your Fire Tablet has a brilliant resolution and an optimal size that you can use to watch movies of all kind. Amazon also provides you with a selection of movies that you can access from the Video Store.

Amazon has tried to solve the problem of buffering by uploading certain movies and shows to its servers that you can directly buy and hence, you don't have to stream these services online but rather you can watch it on the Amazon servers without being annoyed by the buffering.

Buying and Renting videos from Amazon

You can access the Video store by clicking on the Video tab under the Category Bar and clicking on Store. The Video store functions similarly to any other store; you can use the sidebar menu to find movies on the basis of categories or by using the search box at the top.

You can click on a thumbnail to expand the selection and get details about the movies such as watcher reviews, IMDb rating, actor names, etc. You will also see an option to watch the trailer when you click on a movie.

You also have a Watchlist in the sidebar menu that you can use to save all the videos that you want to watch later on. You can add a video to the Watchlist by clicking on the Add to Watchlist button that is next to every video.

Rent Video

There are two buttons that are available next to each video; the buy and the rent button. There are certain videos where there is no Rent button which means that video is not available for renting. If you click on one of these buttons then the price of that video will be charged to your one-click payment option.

You can rent videos from Amazon because they cost less than buying a video and you can watch the rented video which will become unavailable to your after twenty four hours. The twenty four hours don't start till you actually click on the video and start watching it.

Watching Videos

When you buy a video from the Video Store then it is not stored on your device but it is actually streamed to you with the help of your Wi-Fi.

If you want to watch a video then click on that Video in your Video Library or you can use the Watchlist in the sidebar menu. You will see the video player controls by simply clicking on the screen while you are watching a video; you can use these controls to stop, pause, fast forward or change the volume. You can also use the video scrub bar to drag your fingers across it in order to skip from one part of the movie to another.

Download Video

You can download a movie to your device, so that you can watch it later on when you are not connected to a wireless network. Just go to your Video Library and then tap the thumbnail of that video so that you can see the option of Download which will download the movie to your device.

You will then see the option of downloading the movie in HD or SD format; you should pick HD only if you have sufficient storage space in your device or if you only like to watch movies in high resolution. You can watch a downloaded movie as you would watch a movie that you stream.

Streaming from 3rd Party Sites

You can also use third party sites such as Netflix to watch movies. You can use these third party sites by downloading their apps from the Amazon Store and you can then make in-app purchases to subscribe to such third party sites.

You can also use sites such as YouTube or Vine with the help of the Silk Browser but the Silk Browser does not support Flash so it is better to download the app for such sites.

Watching Movies on TV

There are two basic ways that you can use to watch Amazon Videos on your TV.

Second Screen: This feature of Amazon let's you stream the movie that you bought on your Fire Tablet on your Amazon Fire TV or PlayStations with the help of Wi-Fi.

You can use second screen to watch the movie on a larger screen and use your tablet as a remote to control the TV screen. You can activate this feature by clicking on the **Second Screen** icon in the movie player menu on your Tablet.

Display Mirroring: This feature on your Fire Tablet allows you to mirror the screen of your Tablet on your compatible TV, Google Chromecast or Fire TV Stick.

You can mirror the screen of your Fire on your TV by turning on the device you want to display the screen on and then making it 'discoverable' so that your Fire tablet can find the device. You can make it discoverable by using the guide that came with the device; you have to do this because there is no other option but to wirelessly connect your tablet.

- Go to the Settings menu on your tablet,
- Click Display
- Click on Display Mirroring.
- Search for the devices around you,

- Select the device you want to display the screen on
- Click on connect

You can also use an HDMI Dongle which comes with Google Chromecast or Fire TV to wirelessly use Display Mirroring.

Chapter 9:

PHOTOS AND DOCS

The Fire HD Tablet comes with two brilliant cameras, one on the front and the second on the rear of your device, that can be used to capture some stunning pictures. Further, you can use your tablet to manage these photos and work with different documents.

Front-Facing Camera

Using the Camera

Click on the camera app in the apps grid to open and use the two cameras. You can switch between the two cameras by clicking on the button at the bottom with two arrows; the front facing camera looks towards your face while the rear camera is at the back of your tablet and looks in the opposite direction.

Rear-Facing Camera

Basic Function

If you want to take a photo then click on the Shutter icon and it will be automatically saved to your device. You can even see the recent photos that you took in a strip across the bottom part of the Camera app. You can toggle between displaying the film strip and hiding it by clicking on the film strip icon. You can delete photos by tapping on the photo in the film strip and clicking on

59

delete. You will then see an option that says Also Delete from your Cloud Drive which would completely erase the photo from existence and remember that all your photos are saved in the device so even if you delete it from the device you can still access it from the cloud.

Camera Settings

You can click on the camera settings gear to change the configuration of your camera; you can find the gear on the upper right corner of the screen. You can use the toggles here to change the various settings of your camera such as allowing HDR which increases the quality of your photos and is only available for the rear facing camera.

You can go to the camera roll by clicking on the back button in the navigation bar while you're using the camera app. You can use the camera roll to share your pictures, edit them, or even delete them.

You can use the settings menu in your camera app to activate Image Review and it just shows each image you have taken so you can decide whether want to delete or keep it. You'll be asked to review every time that you take pictures with your camera. You can hide the settings menu by swiping upwards.

You can change the settings to determine if you want to save every photo that you take on the Amazon Cloud or not. You can do this by swiping from left to right when you're in the camera roll, swiping down and tapping on Settings; you will see the option to turn Auto-Save on or off in his menu.

Videos: You can also record videos with the help of your rear facing camera if you want by clicking on the red record button. You can zoom in by pinching and even change the volume at which the video is being recoded. You can stop the recording by clicking on the video icon again.

Panorama: You can use this feature to take a long photo by dragging your phone horizontally or vertically to cover more area.

You can use this feature by going to the settings in the camera app and clicking on Panorama.

Click on the capture button and then drag your tablet horizontally or vertically to cover the area you want in the panorama.

Transferring Pictures and Documents

You can mostly use your email to share small documents or files with your other devices but if there is some album or file collection then you will have to use some other techniques.

There are two ways that you can use to transfer files from your Fire to other devices.

USB Transfer: This is the simplest method that you can use; just take a USB Cable that you can use to connect your Fire with a computer. If you use a Mac then should download the Android file transfer application on your computer first. You just have to open the external hard drive folder that you would now be able to see on your computer, go to internal storage or external storage (depending on where you have stored the files) and select the files you want to transfer by browsing through the various folders that you can now see.

You can drag things from your computer and put them anywhere in the internal storage or external storage folder of your Fire. You don't have to select the right folder to paste the item in because your Fire will do that for you.

Cloud Drive: You can install the Amazon cloud on your desktop and then you can simply upload documents to the Amazon cloud or download them.

You can download the Cloud application from the Amazon website. Go to the drop down menu under Your Account and you will see the option of Your Cloud Drive and then simply download the application from there.

Working with Docs

Office Suite: The Docs app that you can find in the apps grid can be used to perform all the basic functions that the Microsoft Office performs. Open the app and then click on the plus icon in the upper right corner. You will see a popup menu from where you can select document, spreadsheet, or presentation depending on the kind of document you want to make.

You can also download various Office Suite apps from the Amazon Store.

Wireless Printing: You can use the print option to wirelessly print anything in Office Suite documents, Camera Roll, or email. Your Fire automatically detects all emails in the vicinity and connects with them. You can use this feature to print stuff directly from your tablet with the help of Wi-Fi.

Business Productivity: You can use your tablet to connect with the intranet of your work place. You can do this by downloading an Office Productivity app from the Amazon Store and then using it to submit expense reports, timesheets, etc.

Creating and Deleting Folders

You should use a brilliant little app known as ES File Explorer to create and delete folders on your Fire Tablet. This app can be used to create folders, sort them, change their position, transfer them, and even delete them.

You can get the app from the Amazon App Store.

Other Doc/Pic Functions

Sending PDFs: If you want to send or read a PDF then you will have to convert it to the AZW format of your Fire HD. You can convert a file by simply sending an email to your Amazon account and writing convert into the subject line while attaching the PDF file. This will automatically convert the file to AZW format so that you read it or even convert it while sending it to someone else.

Taking Screenshots: You can take a screenshot at any time of your display screen by pressing down on the power button and the upper volume button simultaneously. You will hear a small shutter sound if you have successfully taken a screenshot and you can view the screenshot by going to the Photos app in the Apps grid.

Saving web Images: If you find an image while surfing the web that you want to save to your device then press and hold on the image till a small menu appears. You will see the option to Download Image on this menu and all you have to do is click on it. You can view the image in the Photos app that can be found in the Apps grid.

Chapter 10:

TROUBLESHOOTING

Wi-Fi Connections

Wi-Fi connections not working properly can cause a lot of problems and can be disruptive in the normal functioning of your Tablet. If you are not able to connect with a Wi-Fi network then it may be because you entered the wrong password or if the other network has MAC Filtering. This means that the network owner has to add you as a user before you can find and use their network.

If you are facing a bad network connection then you can solve it clicking the power button to turn your tablet off and then on again. This will automatically stop and start all networks to which you are connected. You can also try to restart your tablet to solve this problem.

Fire HD Hangs

You can't really do much if your Fire HD hangs and the only option that you will be left with is restarting your tablet. You can do this by pressing and holding the power button for twenty seconds; make sure that you do this when no USB cable is connected to your device.

If this doesn't solve the problem then try charging it for some time and then again restarting with the help of the power button.

Battery Issues

Battery Issues can range from slow charging to things like battery running out really fast. You can deal with all of these issues by simply conserving your battery by using your tablet optimally.

Your tablet might be charging slowly because you are running too many apps on your Tablet, make sure that you close all apps after you are done using them and try not to use your tablet while it's charging.

In addition, it's important to avoid over charging because this reduces the efficiency of your battery. If your tablet has been charged completely then unplug the charger as soon as possible because overcharging can drain the life from your batteries.

If your battery is running out then you can solve that problem by preserving your battery life. Firstly, use the Sleep Mode option so that your Fire is not consuming battery while you're not using it. You can activate the Sleep Mode by pressing on the power button when you are not using your Tablet and then again pressing it to wake your Tablet up.

You can also set your Fire up so that it goes to sleep after staying idle for a certain period of time. Go to Settings, then power and then tap on the Display Settings to pick the time gap you want before the Fire goes to sleep.

There are various other small tips that you can use to make sure that you don't run out of power such as keeping the brightness low when you don't need it, keeping Wi-Fi and Bluetooth off when you don't need them and using headphones instead of the speakers while watching videos or listening to music.

Travelling Overseas

You have to understand that different countries use different kinds of plugs for charging and these plugs have different voltages. You should check the voltage configurations of the country that you are travelling to so that you can make sure that you have an adapter or smart charger which can fit in the plugs there and can handle the voltage.

You should also try to download as much content as you can store on your Fire before you go out of the country because it can be rather difficult to find Wireless connections in an unfamiliar country.

Extended Warranties

Your Fire typically comes with a one year warranty but you have various options to extend your warranty with the help of third party service providers. You can do this by going to Shop in the Category Bar and then to the Kindle Store where you can find these third party warranty providers.

You will find various warranties such as the option to secure your kindle against electric failure, breakage, or even accidents. You should read everything that is included in the warranty before you sign up for it.

Online Help and Amazon Help

The Fire Help Home Page can be found on the Amazon website and there is even a Help app that can be found in the apps grid. This app or even the Amazon website helpline is really helpful as you have one-on-one chats with Amazon customer service, you can read and watch tutorials, find threads which have similar queries and have been solved and read Amazon and user guides.

Amazon has been using a customer service technique known as Mayday that allows the Amazon representative to connect to your tablet with the help of screen sharing. This means that the Amazon rep can tell you what to do by navigating the tablet for you. They show you what they are doing so that you can also see and learn by drawing on your tablet so that you can see exactly where they are doing and what they are accessing.

You can even search your query on the internet and you will find various forums that can help you to solve your problems such as Mobile Read, Kindle Boards, etc. You should be careful of what you read on the internet. Also, make sure that the answers are for your device and not the earlier versions of Kindle since these devices are considerably different from each other.

Chapter 11:

ACCESSORIES TO ENHANCE YOUR EXPERIENCE

There are various accessories that are available with Fire and there are some that can be bought that will enhance your experience so that you can fully enjoy your Tablet. There are some accessories that have to buy to use your tablet and there are some which just help you to have more fun with your tablet.

Covers, Skins

Covers for your tablet are supposed to protect it when it falls and even protect the body from things like dirt. You should absolutely buy a cover as soon as you get your tablet because you never know when your tablet might slip from your hand and fall.

If you are buying a cover then make sure that you buy one that fits your device and is specifically made for it. There are some covers that come with stands which can be quite effective in balancing your tablet while you are watching a movie or playing a game.

Skins have become the trend for electronic devices; skins are stickers that you can paste around your tablet to change the body and to make it appear better. You have to make sure that the skins you buy are compatible with your device and remember that skins cover your entire device including the back and the front.

Stands

There are certain covers that come with small stands attached to the back and if your cover does not have a stand then you can always buy one. Stands are really important because then you don't have to hold your tablet upright while you're watching a movie or playing a game; stands make it easier to handle your device.

Stands come in a lot of designs such as travel stands, folding, rigid and there are even ones with different angles. Stands are a must if you want to use your device easily instead of having to hold it upright every time you want to do something.

Car Attachments

There are certain accessories that will help you to use your tablet while you're in the car and will make your life easier. You can buy a Car Seat Tablet Holder that can be attached to the back of the front seats so that the people sitting in the back seats can put the tablet in the holder and watch whatever they want. This can be helpful if your car does not have a built-in DVD player.

You can also buy mounts that can be attached to the front dash of the car so that you can use your tablet to navigate with the help of GPS.

Screen Protectors

Screen Protectors are a must for anyone with a touchscreen device. There are various screen protectors that you can buy from the Amazon website that can be used to protect your screen from scratches as well as from breaking if your device falls.

Touchscreens can be really delicate but screen protectors make sure that your screen does not break even if the device falls.

Chargers and Adapters

The Amazon Kindle Fire HD tablet comes with a charger and a standard USB cable. The charger is pretty efficient and can charge the device to completion in almost four hours.

You can also buy a charger that fits into the power source of your car so that you can charge your tablet while you are driving.

There are also adapters that you might want to buy and their main purpose is to help attach the USB cable and charger to any power source. This will come in handy if you are travelling outside the country since the power sources used overseas can be different and it'll also help to connect the USB cable of your Fire with other devices.

CONCLUSION

Hope this book has helped you setup and use your Kindle Fire HD seamlessly and enabled you to enjoy this powerful device.

Continue on with your wonderful journey with this smart device. Hope your doubts are removed and your life has eased. Since this is only the beginning, you will find more comfort and happiness with Kindle Fire HD as you get more fluent with the device and the interface.

Wish you all the best automation possible in your life!

Did you Like this Book?

Let everyone know by posting a review on Amazon. Just click here and it will take you directly to the review page.

And if want to learn some real DIY hack on your new Kindle Fire HD do get in touch at <u>kindletechgames@gmail.com</u>

REFERENCES

Amazon.com

MakeUseOf

Dummies

CNET